ANARCH.

FUTUREPOEM BOOKS
2012

ANARCH.

Frances Richard

Copyright © 2012 Frances Richard
ISBN: 978-0-9822798-7-8

FIRST EDITION | FIRST PRINTING

This edition first published in paperback by Futurepoem books
P.O. Box 7687 JAF Station, NY, NY 10116
www.futurepoem.com

Executive Editor: Dan Machlin
Managing Editor: Jennifer Tamayo
Additional Editors: Chris Martin & Ted Dodson
Guest Editors: Wayne Koestenbaum, Lytle Shaw, Anne Waldman

Cover design: Everything Studio (www.everythingstudio.com)
Typesetting: Mary Austin Speaker (www.maryaustinspeaker.com)
Typefaces: Times Semibold (Spine & Back Cover); Caslon (Text)
Cover image: Ian Parker, Evanescent Light Photography, http://parkerlab.bio.uci.edu/evlight.htm

Printed in the United States of America on acid-free paper

Quote on back cover and in front matter is from the Penguin Classics edition
of John Milton's *Paradise Lost* (2.988-90).

This project is supported in part by the New York State Council on the
Arts with the support of Governor Andrew Cuomo and the New York
State Legislature, as well as by individual donors and subscribers.
Additional support was provided by a Face Out grant, funded by The
Jerome Foundation and administered by The Council of Literary
Magazines and Presses. Futurepoem books is the publishing program of
Futurepoem, Inc., a New York state-based 501(c)3 non-profit
organization dedicated to creating a greater public awareness and
appreciation of innovative literature.

Distributed to the trade by Small Press Distribution, Berkeley, California
Toll-free number (U.S. only): 800.869.7553
Bay Area/International: 510.524.1668
orders@spdbooks.org
www.spdbooks.org

ACKNOWLEDGEMENTS

I'll Drown My Book: Conceptual Writing by Women, ed. Caroline Bergvall,
    Laynie Browne, Teresa Carmody, and Vanessa Place, Les Figues Press,
    2011: The Separatrix
6x6 no. 20 spring 2010: Rooms 1-4 in XIII Parts
Antennae no. 10, February, 2009: Gravitropic, The Separatrix
Woodland Editions chapbook series, 2008: *Anarch.*
*Figuring Color: Kathy Butterly, Felix Gonzalez-Torres, Roy McMakin, Sue
    Williams,* ed. Jenelle Porter and Jeremy Sigler, ICA Boston, 2012: Thing Ire
Rational/Irrational (installation at MoMA PS1, 2010): Tiny Microphone

Thanks to the editors of these publications—Caroline Bergvall, Laynie Browne,
Teresa Carmody, and Vanessa Place, Matvei Yankelevich, Jesse Seldess, Jeremy
Sigler, Brian Teare and Jaime Robles—and to Brian Conley, Rob Fitterman,
Alan Gilbert, Genine Lentine, G.E. Patterson, and Eirik Steinhoff. Thanks to
Futurepoem staff: Dan Machlin, Chris Martin, Mary Austin Speaker, Jennifer
Tamayo and Ted Dodson, and to Futurepoem guest editors 2010-2011: Wayne
Koestenbaum, Lytle Shaw, and Anne Waldman.

...thus the Anarch old,
With faltering speech and visage incomposed,
Answered: "I know thee, stranger, who thou art—"

—PARADISE LOST II, 988-90

CONTENTS

GRAVITROPIC

Light sifting therm

by therm,
turning the dirt on—< greater than or less than >

To weigh down
a place in sanity with muscle ballast, scrabble

into hard rock, katabasis. That noise

is rain. *Acedia*, the sin of
despair—I love that

Racemes eke
up, radicles dig down. They know to breathe
and do it. Just as bacteria

push tenderly, the dead thing turning   again
to radical sugars of the time-drip
salivate it out   again

free-form in scree/the brain dissolves   again
to shapely sugars of the
un-, partially, or hazardously

polluted ground. Heaves and extends

by strong-force fiat back, reloaded
like a platinum–plated skull
in two directions

                : lava
                : Northern Lights

Difficulty, dendrites, fibers, YET—rain—your brain isn't drunk
yet on the liquor of difficulty it distills periodically for some
reason.

"That juice is
justice." These are
undergarments, stripes & little flowers. Weak force, when folding laundry

to fondle around/abraded by
hot ligament sugar, stress of pheromones.
Circumnutation moves the morning glory. Trajectories grope

into the weave

of oft-washed t-shirt

A gleaming fuselage, the tips of all their
spears, out in the agribusiness valley

a sprocket flicker

driving regimented rows, we are inside
a filmic nocturne and the gridded orchard

fades, gray oranges
barely there among gray leaves, and on the horizon

the chemical-plant fire floats in the frame
of rearview mirror inside the frame

of rear windshield, recentering, towering
allée to allée, unphotographably

black, aflare baroque

Melted, fused, remelted, igneous, messed-up, sedimentary, inherited, remedial,
   feel-good, long-range

                              : *gravitropic*
                              : *heliotropic*

Thesis being bionic super-
parts. Like love, a pent-up
tingle like a warhead for accomplishing

supreme. But only via
capillary twitch. A barometric
headache frilled

with sex around the edge

Jackhammer. Took love

and squeezed it, wrote with the syrup
on the friable concave lining
of my forehead. Soft, powdery, fungal, glowing like a cloud, thin tain

of a pocket mirror made from self-glued layers of fresh ice or
desert quartz, old lamina
of sugar

> : *wrote what?*
> : *all-dimensional inscription*

Who fabricated

justice, all-dimensional inscription, two-way glass, if not
evolution at the same time making
rocks? In the eye blink

or tiny apnea between breaths.

Going fearlessly.
"Comparable
to the experience of a mute person tasting sugar"

Micron-thick
spiral growl
at the edge.

A turbine milling

< greater than or less than >

sugar in products. To remove
all valves & tunnels from the earth
would be like expunging language from the mind. To write "earth": faintly

grandiose. "Mind": same.

"Geological, all too geological."

"Love" is worse. Aflare

and so preoccupy with sifting

through two screens, as if to distinguish
rapture (being seized)
from ecstasy

(being outside)

HEALTH INSURANCE

—a little black hole formed &

quickly evaporated. Buying CDs

from the Used World bin

let's have a new

history, because I

want that.

Want a loop contemplation loop. Discrepancy—

don't clench

around the way it looked with my hands when I touched it

Apprehending body-of-lost-nipple pleasure

-lissment, x-light apprehending

through pores in the eyebeam careening

off a number of
               a quantity
                       of a various
         to be born—
                              the eucalyptus hill. Oily molecules

crash to haze, detach

from protective mist—Thoreau

talks about it, how it smudges off, takes your thumbprint, he meant

the silvery sunshade dusted

onto apples & blueberries. Prehistoric walkers (AT-ATs) lifting

containers red, blue, gray, at the Port of Oakland. Emit

midrange gray pearl

Mentholated fog a sudden jet I don't mean wistful raw, mean dangerous

micromuck. Ensnare

its nuclei my

          —difficult rush, swerve

of electric fluid, reading dark

as plenum pressing uterinely

Paradigmatic contour inculcate a double/vestigial lung.

Constricted, cornerless, its region

of perma-sad. Its lightness

of new air inside a sac that bleeds—hyperbolic somewhat

to assert, though things

of the world do bleed ("world" is

worse)—bluish-black sac

attached at the rib

bleeds

sunset

as two-folds an overpower-cloud emitting

you to stain a para-me. True

or false: part of a car's engine

is called harmonic balancer. (True.)

Bullets were too expensive, so they clubbed them to death.

(True.)

The great thing about negativity is it's

consistent.

PREFIX	ANALOG VALUE	DIGITAL VALUE
p (pico)	10^{-12}	–
n (nano)	10^{-9}	–
μ (micro)	10^{-6}	–
m (milli)	10^{-3}	–
k (kilo)	10^{3} (1,000)	2^{10} (1,024)
M (mega)	10^{6} (1,000,000)	2^{20} (1,048,576)
G (giga)	10^{9} (1,000,000,000)	2^{30} (1,073,741,824)
T (tera)	10^{12} (1,000,000,000,000)	2^{40} (1,099,511,627,776)

Skin of right-now scunging over, car

that won't turn over a voice of grinding

hope in a thingness field

I had this friend who shamed me

publicly for liking beauty—

As if to go through that phase

of reciting weeds' beautiful names.

Dear Mother of the

Volunteer Sunflower in vacant lots, Little Sister

of the Weeds

I dare you, turbulent

bitch

A shock. To feel unease

at a word-as-action packet like "response."

So pearly

everlasting,

indian

paintbrush,

queen

anne's

lace is wild

abortifacient, which Dr. certainly knew

but doesn't say. The actual properties

"taking the field by force."

So camp out

in case a time-space tremor

called "what happened" needs your mind. A type

of emit:

dragon ouroboros Viet Nam

lampooned as a belly-scar on Lyndon Johnson.

He pulls his shirt up—

a CO in WWII, Robert Lowell wrote to Father Daniel Berrigan,

"I feel like a dog. I feel

like a son of a bitch."

Evaporate.

& how we are humans now

in a human invention penetrating

far-flung shredded cloud.

Insalubrious

experience of trying to know the fronded diesel-friendly sedge

in effluent

Is ever not inured

against basic fault. Then

in the Bank of America, press

    ☐ audible silence
    ☐ remote annunciator
    ☐ trouble
    ☐ security acknowledge
    ☐ trouble acknowledge

PROMENADE À LA CROIX DU MONT ROYAL

Gravity, universal
backpack, drags downhill a sensate

packet, neurons,
synaesthesia with contours, finite, able

to die, me, the creature

moving its name on the small domestic mountain
Trillium

and magnolias are in bloom
Slice a tranche

of this April with its see-through, it is called
April and functions

like a knife to disembed
ice storm and deep horizon

Gravity paws my shoulders, basic
claw, it is not very much like a monkey

but hangs on, drags the branches
in their temporary chrysalids, forces a plume

up the sea
I try to get

combobulated

Allegedly to pray for people
because you are afraid of them is

right

Inside a person a small vortex of clinamen makes
free will, not a metaphor, a

-tronic flicker

What feeler
to extend into this force-

field whirring, tongue-shaped
stretch-forth of your wanting to—construe—the flurry

of which chemicals arcing
gaps or fusing tissue cushions, little wires

make murder, bloody gobbets
on the window of the bus

"The blue jay will come right into your heart,"
said the roshi, from distances

the car alarm will come right into your heart, not a
fugue but never full stop, as once

the mountainette was a bubble molten

in Ordovician rock. Then
if like most of the rest of you, I was raised

in the twentieth century, how to divide
by a synonym?

How to make, not even the quark
has such small motor skills, as gravity

summons transparency off the contours of matter

The cross on the summit is made of light bulbs
dressing-room-mirror-style, blowsy

glyph for high
transparency, advertise this

way to suffer. Thinking, strange
dearth of graffiti here, the lining of the wind

is ice, it rattles, and about this
drift—

Behailu Bezabih of Addis Ababa, artist and teacher,
tell me if you know.

DRY PLACE

Voluminous

athwart the waveform grasses, serried

"all is well except my head"

adorned with thorns and burrs, with scratches, underbeeps, the issue

fountains, is a fountain; quell it

Look at the sexy rocks

Tissue

of a gray-within-a-gray that swallows shadow, shadow

a visible whisper, whisper

an aural shadow, tall ion cascade

heart-murmur of a nondescript

reactor over there, i.e. the person

who reacts as would-be

mammal with a chakra left ajar

Wet appearance

a very hot day. Stillness

coating leaves

dark & cleverly heavy, a condor

midday's minion

is

inhuman. The madrone

exfoliating

Sensors, in the Safeway parking lot, register imagined

constellations. Handling berries

in their ♻1 boxes, distinctive

sound of the boxes, transparent

brittle tinkling like gasoline

I want

you will serve as a basic exemplar

of the sentence

a skitter in

folds of starlight, interstellar musk-gland warble

of coyotes' twenty voices printing

Os in our spinal fluid as you record

their distances handheld, fire flaring

as I mispour tequila out as water

IMPLEMENT

In that I like
it   am consoled, if a person makes

a species of mistake
we are the species   evolved to cry O

help
though bears etc. inebriate   what let's implement a metaphysic

to quickly term
themselves   on fermenting berries

and tiny frogs
swim in the pitcher plant's raindrop   croak their decibels

as proof

You are so | | | | | | | | | | | | | | |
Make the world elastic   with a rose nimbus, like sexual flesh

oof, ça soulage, he said, throwing the brick

I was trying to realize plain
thrill as effable   but plus

malfeasance, topple, pervasive
unsatisfactoriness, heat-death. It crashed   so? Counter-/punching

technoscape
O Death

I too dislike it

Restful old-lady boredom
on the uncrowded bus, proximate   "riot of flowers"

The hero punched
a rock with a superlative fist   In a billow

of the pulverized occurred more
carnal and widespread mind-breaking   in the cleft. Yet too

quiescent, compulsively
release, step   out in the superlative again

proximate to the bank
and forget to be grateful for money performing obedient | | | | | | | | | | | | |

from the slot

under-nascent
surge   as if mine like water

What is the arcanum
at its uncost   utmost level

a little panic
who was   double-helical

the "platform"

THE SMEAR

[plunged]

Maybe I just always need
a weevil in the flour. A canker? Yeah, the smear, it's called the
small other object

My little ah, ah, excess, stain—

Go toward it.

As in sci fi?

Yeah, zoom

in to rot and a sluglike body, protuberant tumor, find it armored, a
stormtrooper, gobs gelatinous & tarry, iron nub or clinker kernel, lewd sprawl
of Agent Orange or nano-plume of organ-gnawing grit

inside that is a paradisal garden

inside that milk & honey struck perpetual from the rock, inside that every
scratched old-vinyl Beatles record, inside that sex, inside that not-too-sweet
rice pudding, inside that clean sheets on a dark night

cacophonous/diaphanous with stars—

Did you forget diaphany

temporarily?

I did. I plunged

[*hex lining*]

A lining sheathing

fleck-like, sac-shaped shimmer or flint splintered &

cooperatively dreamed

a rustling, sometimes painful

silver like the burning

edge of vapor or a cheap silk camisole or a green

of nervous chlorophyll in baby leaves against black twigs or spectrum slick

or black ice or the smear

of marzipan under the crust or halo of ache

burning on a wound about an hour after cutting

with the bread knife accidentally not on purpose or the feeling

of *if* or *or* or vast sums

of confusing positions & their crisscross or how you cannot

fuck your way back to the womb or wanting the phone to ring

but it persists inert, dumb, or the anonymous

face of the protestor with green headscarf

What conjecture

regarding her or tendencies is a sheath, a scrim

imbued on the inner

side, the

brain side, with how she lived a baby once

absorbing from her mother's pattern daily, or her mother

died or disappeared but someone

spoke, she learned, and aren't there leptons

whose job is blip-perennially to quake? How presume

though they bombard I assume extremely

frequently, "every instant" "I" have nada contour

plus this wrinkle is glassy cloth/insanely fine-spun winding-sheet

of hum, can never taste

or stroke the lining of the inside of the lining—

"myelin sheath" was a hit

when I told them about it

it sleeves the nerves. But couldn't ever, not enough & don't your furies

cross the whole

"space-mama, time-mama" *basta ya* who shoved

a radioactive grain or homing device

breach the membrane

her fearlessness

with surging other people in that avenue, & forces

who behoove an entry-spot, infiltrator who could turn

again to be the splash of very wild—

you who are ice-luminous.

So non, a miniscule overplus

to make the gap between honey and charmed honey. Opine

a quantum crust of incantation

binding honey-drops, arabesque

of hex, important parts

of everything as mouthfuls of invisibility

[*non-metaphorical furnace*]

But I mean dark. Widening gyre of the ilk

of interstellar howl where *echthroi* streak

as subatomic cold or tearing holes, one

jagged rip in the stickiness that cleaves together matter as if it were easy

to say "matter," like that incestuous

old man—last year, it's true, he showed me

an eagle's nest in a pine tree

by the lake—but now—or the patient voice on-air

of a man, he sounded young, who stood in a pit of water

stood in a pit of water

stood in a pit of water

squatted in a pit

of water stood in a pit

in a pit of water

of water and piss

stood in a pit of water

with bars above

a pit in the ground

in the rain

stood in a pit

of water in a pit of water stood as it filled

with many I think it was fifty

men who stood in the pit with him

they pissed and bled and if they leapt up to hang on the bars

soldiers stamped on their hands, they hoisted them

out to shit then pushed them back, they cut

him, and he spoke on the radio

in a soft, patient, matter-of-fact, clear voice

Is it not even interesting

Claw of repulsive

& voluptuous unmaking swiped through the flesh of things,

blood of the other mind

through the flesh of the mind?

Is stimuli not

active with a stutter of the replicative

—here

re-do—fierce muttering—because it gnaws

like mold on the fruit/on the meat of how

humans act? Actually not

flora-decay or organ-heat but like a plume

of eerie-perfected shriek. White phosphorous

dump. Like sin—

A holocaustic little furnace leaping

A non-metaphorical pit

[*the charge*]

No. I meant to mean
the other dark. Transect

the smear: "describe difference
by describing edge." As the leper said, "You. Name

a few beautiful things."

TINY MICROPHONE

then I said to my soul,

,,

and my soul said I canopy language

and a further   over, rubber soul translated   simultaneously, like

a dadaist   ,,,   at the U.N.
        ,,,
          ,,
            ,,

species rage   langurage

as baby-rage   at the gone total   milk bauble

exactly   not a free force   on the high place what is exact

craved my third soul, testify

,,,
,,,
,,,
,,,

inside assemblage   ,,,,,,,,,,,,,,,,,,,,,,,,,,,,,,,,   before concatenate, like
,,
,,
,,,

milk in a mirror?   because the   mossy rock cleaves

ur-minutely   ,,,,,,,,,,,,,,,,,,,,,,,,,,,,,,,,,,,,   and spores accept

,,
,,
,,

my thought averred its organism traveled

scant wander   intercalculate the woods   and term mitosis

crystal cleavage, rate of   expansion   rhizomatic gist

what the cells do   you guys sure do excel   evinced my

half-formulated   ,,,,,,,,,,,,,,,,,,,,,,,,,,,,,,,,,,,,,,,   coexist
                             ,,
          ,,
                        ,,

and tenderly the

plethora   occurred more   I felt their

shapes, leaf-rot   sticky-foot, breeze, igneous, miles, we suck   at it I said

their   trembling equivalenced   susurrus, crack *well* ,,,

,,,

consciousness

,

a problem arose

with exquisite beauty,,

,,
,,
,,,

punctum blue laser

I could hear the freeway
gathered ,,,
,,
,,,
,,

in the tiny microphone

HARD SYRUP (GRAVITROPIC OUTTAKES)

Hard syrup/sludge, pitch sap

precipitates   is milked out
                                sweated from
                                exuded by

"the past."
Deep time, thick
description spread

at high rheology.
Sub rosa sub-
trench.

Death, sugar, justice. Or

part-animal
made of mercury, incarnate
chlorophyll. Two hot spots

pull the monad: Molten
in the earth, molten
in the sky. Come down on you. Hard

if a cyborg-coyote-flower job is to lick
fur backward, suck fervent
crude back down the mile's neck.

That which occurs, or

trembles and jiggles like jello, like a hummingbird, cytoblast.

as sparks fly upward, or:

In the ignimbrite caldera brown as cake
beneath the greening sunrise.
Every minute during which

we were talking about the failure of basic love, a compacted reeking layer
of dead leaves, burnt foil, newspapers, and plastic
—"all language has a molding effect

on plastic reality"—tiny gun
or princess's pink battle-axe—continued slowly in all directions
to modify.

You said,
"I wasn't really capable
of listening to you then."

"How about now?"

"I'm trying—"

As lactose, glucose, maltose, dextrose, fructose, especially honey & cellulose are
     mellifluous
& specific, they hold
the trees up.

As this syrup of your density
is oval.
As mouth is

oval, in the middle changeable,

but finite at the edge.

THE SEPARATRIX

de vez en cuando

the political

a blank
A QUALITY.

        absurdity, suffering, volatile
HA!, a blank, a quality, resentment, crushing
grief, to grieve again, they shot him again. Malaise: a skeptical: erase: the people

who leave AC on all night when it, the humid wind, is actually cool. Exhalation
of charcoal/green leaf-ruffling off water, over empty land, with ticking engines
and radiating concrete alleviating. Cool. A man in a hood behind barbed wire

comforting his son. A

woman
fainting, obviously with grief, and the hands of another woman out of frame
that hold her forehead as if she were vomiting.

ah ah aha ah ah ach ach ah blah ach blah ah ach ach blah blah blah blah blah blah ha ha ha ha ha ha ha ha ha ha ha ha ha ha ha ha ha ha ha ha ha ha ha ha ha ha ha ha ha ha ha ha ha ha ha ha ha ha ha ha ha ha ha ha ha ha no ach blah blah blah blah blah blah blah blah blah blah blah blah blah blah blah blah blah blah blah blah blah blah blah blah blah ⟶

⬇

»»»

blah blah blah blah blah blah blah blah blah blah blah blah blah blah blah blah blah blah blah blah blah blah blah blah blah blah blah blah blah blah blah blah blah blah blah blah blah blah blah blah blah blah blah blah blah blah blah blah blah blah blah blah blah blah blah blah blah blah blah blah blah blah blah blah blah blah blah blah blah blah blah blah blah blah blah blah blah blah blah blah no blah blah blah blah blah blah blah blah no blah blah blah blah blah blah blah blah blah blah blah …

...blah blah blah blah blah blah blah blah blah blah blah blah
blah blah blah blah blah no no no no no no no no no blah blah blah blah blah
blah blah blah blah blah blah blah blah blah blah ha ha ha ha ha ha ha ha ha ha
ha ha ha ha ha ha ha ha ha no ha no ha ha

↓   ↓ ↓   ↓

ha ha ha ha ha ha ha ha
ha ha ha ha ha ha ha ha ha ha ha ha ha ha ha ha ha no ha ha ha ha ha ha ha
ha ha ha ha ha ach ha ha ha ach

That is YOUR SON. He is about five. There is barbed wire, ergo somewhere
guns. He can't see your face, you can't see
his. Familiar

shape of his bones under your hands. What befell,
do you suppose, that woman? It concerns
her son, her guns, nature

made it so everyone remembers how vomiting feels. We try to avoid it.

The AC's job is to change the air. We don't like how it is.

Rage, legion, water cannon, bulldoze, blaze, a spray-paint, laugh, red pulse, old
inhuwomanity of guts. The mosses flick
all pattycake, osmosis loves a pata-permeable
node through this? Wince, not notice. Make a cushy place. Gods
in archaic stories often laugh,
not compassionately but from the seat of power.

Q: Who is yr. lover?
A: Why do you ask?
A: The Separatrix.

Mosses dripping, cush, wee curlicues and dewy horizontal
cunt of the rockface. Couch
of the perfect entropic, no snow in uncanny
New England. A climate's job
is to change the air and wash it
over/into what is there.

I'm telling you. The cormorant/computer
yawns, new phrasal holes arrive more smoothly from the
ether/gullet placed into our cerebellar umbral
orifice & ahead of the outline-ghost
in immaterial sequins, since all humans
love a human face like my child—

From the broad world, then, more: *justice* is expected?

Let's think.

Unloving-behavior magnet: miscalculation: the Law. This man is a position

billowing from his irritable body, collapsing veins, thrown up, feet tender and

blood(s)hot addict-

hood,

from under this

hood: If he were stripped

of the cloud.   This cloud:

of panicky deca-tele-hypnocluster, green ache, a seasick
trillions swarming gnaw his head/it pinches
to tell blood-oxygen his finger. In the gnash™
sweat shadow, pointed salts, notorious cracking
lump beneath his jacket. Wire jerks him. Homunculus
worried cowering remote begrims
his forehead, burning the cloud ≠ him. The cloud

flat! FLAT! collapsing

sucked into my lights seared tile spores & smartdust tracks me, *il est*
blow-back, reuptake geysering, drowns lungs & gauze pads on aporiae
as intake can't be filters. Polyparticulator grinding in a slurry, hyper-
sharpened screen CAUTION: HOT eye chirping eye chips threshes
me, loves me a plume of giga-tera–fog each grain sobbing
uncontrollably with angular numbers coughing in a pile, stripped
because it wants

it wants my duolaminate. Spray perforates
the scarified mud & orchard, the cloud

gods out from his pointer-finger, bird of portent
entrails hanging gut-shot home to roost.
Due to the fact
the fact that under seal of *roi soleil*–cum–he administered

the shredder all himself, & a shard
of Kryptonite to the frontal cortex.

[put a color on the screen.
Just a soothing one. Hurry. Blank. They measured
chromatic vibration of the universe—thought it
was turquoise, but miscalculated]

[as infinite space?
no, contraintimate, mayhap the other lung, right simultaneous
inside as every quark turbines omni "directionally"—we call them
"directions"]

[in this new life
he is sent to count the drips in a plastic bucket
at the village spigot—he crouches on his hunkers in soft dust
under the shade-tree, children & chickens mock him
mostly kindly, some widow
feeds him alms]

[wimmin
womyn not grrrls—that's a graphic
time mark.]

"said they rule my
/Said"

loved that, wrote ♀ in ballpoint on our
Converse

the lifeworld. "Silence *is*
like starvation, don't be fooled…" "The dream

of a common language…" "The master's tools will never dismantle
the master's house."

I think you would like it
if this archive embarrassed me and if I disavowed it.

OUTLET FIRE

"A garden of medicinal flowers…"

"Cake!"

Such answers help

insofar as how many days

were you a child? Or can you fix it

with your mind, since it did not happen

in your mind? "Time crashes

into words so often."

•

An experienced fire scholar

observes we hold a species monopoly

over fire, fire

is a profoundly interactive technology, yet people

rarely burn as nature burns.

And out of the wilderburbs

we reinstated fire to remedy a longtime

fire famine. An expected major wind event

took place. Light 'em or fight 'em

and shoving biomass around, hazards

of reintroduction of the lost species of

fire resulted quickly

in a 14,000-acre black-and-silverscape

to anneal our eyes. The flicker

folding denuded understory, traversing undone

growth in its slight rise and curve whose carbon plateau

resists, the way we scanned our bodies to fix

I and got a Pleistocene, some shiny

seeps, "a tickle

at the back of the throat"

•

A come-home urge, a short-term

wedding ring or nerve tonic

of conversation in the car

•

Not unintimate

but a claw into the sector

•

In this area where quelling

worked or gracious

tissue has not surged back. To anneal

is to harden, and I was told

so many times to love the killed place

charred, the charnel

and charmed skeleton-of-ghosts place. Appeared moonlit

in daylight and its narrative

was goblin, homeless

burrow, carburetor. Intelligence instigated this

big elegy

•

Conscious

with its retardant like let's live together. But cut by river, worn

by air, détourned by wind like I won't disappear

if the line of wavy green in the non-shatter glass

maintains its vein

in tangibility. If adrenalin splits

chemicals with this sector. Immolated-to-the-

drop-off place that shimmeringly

waits

•

Snags, slash, deadfall, flesh of

charcoal flower burns

urging off the tongue. Leaves a

husk-shape perfect, subject

to astonishing dispersal. So carve a channel

in your voice, go coursing

rockily

along the burned-up hologram of I

make a plan

•

The question had been as usual what is

ultimate? Cake of

burning shimmer in the

woods, your

question had been too much

of the wrong kind of fire and not enough of the right

kind. Apocalypse dryads

without new weeds or saplings to befriend, emollient

tar and failure

medicine. We come through

you, null

quadrant, in our vehicle. And fumes of wanting

to be otherwise escaped

ANIMATION FRAGMENT

Grayscale   off the coast of chaos

                                             in anime
                                             in a graphic novel, hawk-wings
                                             skimming waves of lapping nothing

                                             haggard breastplate
                                             cross-hatched adversary acts
                                             on the dark side
on reconnaissance   p.o.v. on vatic first-person

shooter
fizz or globule
loops absence

vitreous humor
and crystal meniscus cusp
the unfinished logiverse

Musculature of sex   in disillusionment
                                             in shadow, sibilance
                                             grunts, vacuum on the soundtrack
                                             stretch hours, pages flutter,

Graphite boredom
scrolling

Lush
chiaroscuro tool

                               Voilà finally, miniscule
                               speck rears *la tour abolie*, telescopic
                               Brasilia looming, tumbling satellite,

                               brownfields, test site of the Ice Queen
                               Mother Night, villain lair
                               of Chaos in the bowel of the mountain

Shall I be   free, unleash

                               door clangs
                               on the mineshaft in nonentity
                               Palace of disorder parents

brood a recognition scene

whose lynxes glow Chernobyl
whose cowls drape antimatter
whose scripts leak active smoke

Palsy and homing
palpable, far-sighted, we

who sustain the
groundless say go ahead

THING IRE

i.

     The baby said————Ire. It was pushing
sheaths————folding molten————faulting. I cop its mother. Close
to the apex ticklish, inverted, of its tip

————a gifted knot.

The baby's breath————occur————long streams of broken. Fluid
phlegm of underforce, mold/cast of blackening translucent
Herculaneum, a drop
of salty————condensation. Suck a small male spirit
on a wire sticking bent with a recycled————upturn
activate her mouth. Cry as dolls
to move around and————people space. Turned very faintly
pink————a t-shirt washed with crimson
underpants. Erratum, penetralia, the baby's
personality merged out————came definitely
polymer, a smoke, astounding properties
of————balm————of bruisy meat. I gathered

all my baby up and urged her back. "There, there,"

I bade. I said
her————be a zero again, an O

to pour because of————& obediently, she
did

ii.

Spectral paper larded with
emulsion———by some reassign———it never really

clung close to, infiltrated or dyed. Floated separate
through the slither———electrolyte———a honey in a laminate

set-point for worry, glossy finish———empty
case. I opened an earth bracket

in our very yard to eat old arguments, newspapers, & something
parted———ripped free to come

lax. Composed of two

———analyses. The feminist
surges, mirror ashing off the panel

always at the back, a spangle

of jellied force———it clung too urge———&
yearned. Doing sun-tricks.

A shooting———pain rose, fuchsia, black, then white
slapped me across the face———Please

Please

thing isn't———a verb

UNIVERSALLY ACCEPTED DEFINITION

i.

Out of the wind-shirred depth-stripes
in the ocean we could hear

the dolphins cough

Verges of sensate triggered
me, they push

against a membrane quondam toxin, explain
erasing as a way of knowing, tending

to discredit by an act of non-address

Move the object back to cover an unseemly
rip in spacetime, open

portal sucking stellar wind

The idea "instinct-injured"
helped explain, and the rule "reverse the image

of porosity"—feel happy and so violently
porous. "Last night," you said,

"I was killed twice by goblins," and I coalesce
all afternoon as container-ships

from Chinese-painting fog, egg-yolk sun sets
into ashen clouds—I know according

to this cliff. Dolphins insert a character called

space. Beside the freeway in the salt-marsh, two herons
raise white S's

in orange parasitic moss to spell
semi. Dry stellate burrs, the dead computer monitor face down

embracing squelching inter-hummocks. Who brought
lawn chairs, mute tesserae like crashing

through the lilies a swamp-bred prehistoric fish
some nine feet long. Like soapy water emptied

on the ground. How every blade of grass
bends whispering please

please. Their sound performs a cloud of gnats
entrenching in the mist some sun allows

ii.

Who felt upwelling, thought you might
be steep exercise, like a mountain. Lay in bed

in the midst of electricity

and sleeked my muscles and folded my silent brain
to feel the dolphins' surge, which is not

mediate. The question was, is
this a landscape

or a portrait? The answer was phytoplankton blooms
can or used to be seen from space.

The question was "a person
has a billion dollars, so why cannot a mountain

have a billion leaves?"
The answer was there is no universally

accepted definition of "a mountain."

ROOMS 1-4 IN XIII PARTS

i.

Common in/un

modes, registers, go ahead
and send your loving kindness to a
mossy rock—is this

an attribute?   voiceprint
                                 vibeprint
                                 [wish I knew how to knit]

if you turn to
if you go to
if you click

a dizzying trip. Rest
in hesitation. Something like totally
counterteleological collage—

sloppy thinking as good, as a messy come-on. In structural polyvocality, epic
pointing down between the spores, less a tiny
than a near unspace. Compassion

is the hardest human thing.

ii.

What Walter Benjamin carried over the Pyrenees to Spain
was his unfinished mss. i.e. not intending
to overdose poor lamby. What links this/you?
Yes. Yet
yourself not be amidst
a moral imperative to use only
pungently accurate and therefore a rip
in totalitario-imperial shellac over consciousness, i.e. a t-shirt—
ZAUM AS A SECOND LANGUAGE.
As if there were consciousness. Isn't
there? In fact he may have been
assassinated by Stalinists. Someone said
she disapproved of meaning.

iii.

Neighbor/beloved/cousin/parent: thinking: they will
kill you like the stranger. Let's try
to live free of meaning:

[that was thirty seconds—

iv.

—mildly drastic. fluorescent/leak of practice
chaos through the crack in tensor time]
[ammonia soup/farmed pulp/non-union job thus desiccated and hot-rolled as
this page][mechanized
air]
[an alternate unmeaning might be let's consider rooms
wherein the sinews
of personhood claw and hack and are clawed and are hacked, dreck
sprayed intentionally into the eyes of the creature by the creature]
[No. That has meaning.]

.

v.

This conversation made me anxious. Bunkerlike gray effort. Excess of mini-
plastic water bottles curved and grooved
like the baroque. And getting
hangry—

vi.

"Say it. Say it. The universe—"

vii.

Fills, flows, fields, effluvia, of course
sand and slime exist outside of language, the relief of it!
But then of course
their imprint—sweet
wholeness of your masticated cake—i.e. if cake
is sugar/fat/eggs/flour/multiple
petroleum-derived additives/stomach acids/shit/sewage/wheat
and cane in the field/field- factory- trucker- and store-workers, and of course
a craving/memory/the picture moist
and porous as a—what, a kind of sponge for sopping up and wringing out
vomit, consolation, small delight—the mother's body, ultimately? then—
good news! it is never
gone—grit, slime—the monster cake!

viii.

"The child," she said, "who can blow up the world with her thought."
"The killing," she said, "rekilling and superkilling."

ix.

disjecta membra sounds

pretty

like limbs of the scattered god

gobbets fertilizing

x.

oops, *god*. over the Pyrenees.

oft not-okay

but here quasi? polis ticks

full of structure

xi.

Then I said, Black President. She said, "Eileen is my president." She said
Olson that bearish misogynist [she said
Smithson—kind of an asshole] but Oppen and Mary were nice. "Say it, say it"
was said by M. Rukeyser, *The Speed of Darkness*, 1968.

xii.

Dripping sound in the background. Could be
pastoral, poison, or a plumbing
anomaly. Flatline

agitated in sweat-beads in monitor
flare—who watches
this dreck? So could we determine, collectively, which artery

clogged in plaque throbs in the man
who shouted "you lie!" at the president [this is
a narrative] and which in the man [this is a therapy]

who threw his shoes at the president? "To rescue

language-objects from capitalism—"

xiii.

For the next x instants, possess your mind
in freedom from—

I wanted to say concepts. As in "what angel type are you"/never could do
avenging—"concept"

as mental form or empty set, "concept" as
highly stylized self-conscious gesture, "concept"

as susceptible to logical proof as distinct from "idea"
or intimation as in "the *hic et nunc* continuum, the radically

infra-theoretical, orature, or cusp"—I heard a fly buzz
when I lied—as the plastic bottle [readymade][will take approx. 1000 years

to biodegrade] lends molecules
to spaces in the speaker's

flesh—I mean who guards
the guardians? I mean

not me—but a supposed person but not because
there is a diary and

separatio/coniunctio is all we ever
talk about—who takes

this project to be thirst

OUTTAKES

occasional peace

be more

"the character of your daemon is

responsible, solitary, modest, shy, and proud"

timescale in muscle

sonic concussion

walk out into an oncoming wall of sun

softening asphalt like a tar pit, or that time I thought the moonlight

made a sound

and still withstand it, lithe stripe of mid-percussive

lathe of outwash

grinding, churning, filing down

the grassroots justice community temporarily

ingrate, convoluted or trying to have pleasurable friction, coefficient of biolocation

waft between

matter at least is not private

a hundred thousand kalpas is about right

cream, green jasmine tea

Citron Mélisse

potassium, silicate

I thought it said I want to wash the ocean

bend the edges of old trance but that was wrong

a narcissistic

wound I stupidly shrunk

my favorite sweater

contents of purse or pockets, *dans mon sac*

what it's like to have some money

a tocsin, Klaxon, water

or the sweetness of a dog

Kleenex like a used-up dove

frisson

there is no end

there is no end

one version of this only creates happiness

earth-movers across the street

festooned with colored ribbon while demolishing

the notions & trimmings warehouse

your secret history of ye olde dividing line

a dividing line *sans* secrets

as if each person

on the subway could be honored like that guy facing down the tank

HELIOTROPIC

White ink of sun, of outwash, dazzlement, *dépense*, a chemically suspect
froth whipped onshore. Unpigmented
seep deep under—or a runnel on the hard dry—dirt.

Diurnal motion. Parts track. White sink

of sun as flowers
may assume a random glance
in other lights, but at dawn their motor cells on the shadow side

flex.

Want to be
a result here. Body in it—
viability lately—a publicly

unmanageable thought-life.
But I liked what you were saying
about your head…

Heliotropism is response to blue light. Thus, if at night
a heliotropic species is covered with a red transparent cover—
Dry wind with its long lick

over salt flats, archaic lakes, prehistory in
overconfident information. The crystal land
mind-numbing, friable, mobile singing

sand mountain—have a great

flight! don't think about the air. There is a special
blue butterfly. The installation
delivers its estimated 65,000 thoughts per day, of which 90% are

biomechanically speedy & trending

toward the apex. And what price force or chlorophyll
but love, adore a zone inside which pull—a project nominally
accomodationist—

forgivist.

Flesh out "the same."

ANARCH.

August 06 - January 07

[The fairy swamp: apparitions]

The fairy swamp: apparitions
as weed-trees
surrounded by (& this is a common dream-sign

for the self) marshes and rubbish-tips.

A hemmed-in wasteland hurtles
fixed between subdivisions
and the Amtrak track. Empty, persevering

in a live film-strip of scorched
grass: "Not too much sky," the directing voice
cautions the hand on the camera—

Fat clump-shaped snowflakes give up
diverse perfection
in muddy water. Cranberry bog alit

with what water does to color when it hovers, exaggerates
the optics
in a surface magnificat—

[*"Vision maps, history tools, technology, poetry…"*]

"Vision maps, history tools, technology, poetry, and letting
their differences irritate each other."

After the world becomes round, and the agitated
sand-grains darken with spilled oil—

World gathered into a ball. Crushed into a ball.
"Anarch. is an acupuncture point."

Anarch. is a house afloat, the moment
when the train becomes the bridge, and the light the train.

"It is better to say, 'I'm suffering,' than to say
'this landscape is ugly.'"

Right. Or persevering, x-factoring

left x. What can't
be measured, won't recuperate:

the food and sex realm, food and sex and attention
realm, food and sex and attention and flicker realm—

Far-off death village.

High up in circumstance. Pissed off
at circumstance. All around the way you and I

were moving, you and I were standing
still in (a ring of fire) (a lake of fire) (a burning

lake) (a chain)

A woman embroidering on the subway. She weaves a line. A man intent
on the pinging of the screen in his raised hand, flesh curved

around the bones around the phone.

"A semiotic in a way approach"

Tornado over a muck field. Thick black cake frosting, pulsatile
hive. Marshes, rubbish-tips, rusted boondocks, fetid pools
in broken concrete, fungus, mold, smashed glass and riveted trestles,
factories, gantries, bridges, skeletal railways
spilled on sodden ground. Electric green slime (algal bloom/dumped antifreeze)
a blot of color vital on the water.

A plastic bucket at the village spigot. Microeconomically a woman
owns the area cell phone—

& another dream: of gardens, paving stones
alive with rain and crystals. Interpenetrated
backyards choked with hollyhock, vines, pods, arbors
arcing, heliotrope, emerging into rags
of oily brûme. House
subsiding, porch wrenched, wet couches
plaid and turbid. Garbage-bags
burst tumbling down the gully.

"She was mentally insane."

An acupuncture point.

But he said, and I copied: "I should think fire
the best thing in the world
if I were not acquainted with air, and water, and earth."

A gold sky-trick hits Hoboken. Joyous drop
of the helicopter, rotors chopping sleep, the child insists
on calling it "happycopter."

Untwist the energy braid.

[Joyous drop]

Joyous drop
of the helicopter
like the windhover.

But, in an emailed thumbnail peace-
video, the muscled camouflage boy
looks like walking suffering

to me. Thus: please rewind the ocean
to exactly its configuration at the moment
of my/his birth? Please spool

the river backward on its *technê* reel
to the source. Its *arche* reel.
Ex-thunderclap, used

sound incised on the ubiquitous now-cheap
device. What is emulsion
or magnetism but ghostliness

in the real world, what voice
do ones and zeroes have but twittering
bat pings/rustling husks of shades?

So many oblivions
were present when I went there. We fantasize
they (trees) are calm—

There is such a thing as bad
enlightenment. Trees commandeered
to serve as model

sufferers, imperturbable
brawn and grace in multiple weathers.
Mute, hackable, pointy—a sweater

(for example) is a very complex knot. Ruffled and folded
time-space, anarchic
jump between rings or layers, fusing, following one

double weave. Mathematically, a *horned*
sphere, a *wild* sphere. "That raises
a lovely question—"

[*To be burned*]

To be burned. Hyperprocessed
fire jets from its nozzle. Falling
on stony ground, till the stones

are scorched, and the fiberglass skin, and the regular
skin. In the mean
time, I had so much

garbage towards them, tasting it, "then something happens
and the smooth is gone." She understood Time Warner
to be the one who warns us

regarding time. Which might be a)
the monster in *demonstrate*; b) the mother
of emptiness; c) a blanket

apology. "Of what a strange nature
is knowledge! It clings to the mind
when it has once seized upon it, like a lichen

on the rock." Like gelatinous
fire on soil. *Res ipsa loquitur*
was a factoid I learned at dinner, and the skin

hurt. It spoke
in the twitter of nerves about the cause
of its own shrieking—

Curved infinity is different
from straight infinity. I noted that. Venn diagram
of rogue areas, vexed

overlap and reeling the energy
in—or, after
twelve hours of self and other

you need a break. I need. Straight
hours break
into trace flakes of time

that waft on you and cling. On I
they cling, as to the underbelly
of subcutaneous space

as cosmos, the intraquarky layer, which
is alleged to be by nature
blissful—think of it

as a fourth moment: past, present, future, and
ex-thunderclap. Isn't that too
double? As in the rising

of paranormal gentleness, when the soldier
appears in pixels as if dressed in twitching lichen. Glory
x to x for x-ed things, and the terrible axe

chopping at my backbone turns to
heat-haze, water-ripple. Please
be a particle

of this explosion.

[Who commandeered]

Who commandeered
the tree? Who.

Woman knitting on the endless
subway. Reenacting out

a giant hurtling
shade of gray. "For help, see

the disambiguation page."
Q: Have you ever tried

to represent the wind before?
A: I don't think so.

Then I
mini–went through it again. But the page rose up

as a unit of measure for everywhere use.
Page of the primal

breast-as-movie-screen. Page of light partitioning
the distance. Bed-sheet page on which the dream

self-writes, and the drop of spermicide.
Oleaginous

fascia page, bony prominence page, page of
math, page bent

into a tube. Page of sliced trees bleached
and boiled down. I was strewn

by this drift/surge—

The mountain range
was carved from blue polystyrene insulation board. Glittering
in sunlight. Copyrighted

icebergs rise and sink, they waft away, as when the sponsoring logos
& love-advertisements burn away
from the outer skin of the satellite in reentry.

Still, from the point of view of space, the hole
a mile deep in the plateau
whence they dig out useful mineral appears like—

it appears. Anarch.
"*Arche* (αρχ)"

("For help, see—")

"— is the beginning or first principle of the world. The idea was philosophized by Thales of Miletus who claimed that the first principle of all things is water. His theory was supported by the observation of moisture throughout the world and coincided with his theory that the earth floated on water. Thales' theory was refuted by his pupil and successor Anaximander.

Anaximander noted that water could not be arche because it could not give rise to its opposite, fire. Anaximander claimed that none of the elements could be arche for the same reason. Instead, he proposed *apeiron*, an indefinite substance from which all things are born and to which all things return.

Anaximenes, Anaximander's pupil, advanced yet another theory. He returns to the elemental premise, but posits as arche air, rather than water. Anaximenes suggests that all is made from air through rarefaction or condensation. Rarefied, air becomes fire; condensed, it becomes first wind, then cloud, water, earth, and stone in order."

(& flesh in this continuum thickens/or dissolves)

[*Corrosive leak*]

Corrosive leak from the too-loud
t.v., page of scrolling light.

Pundit meddling with a drowning
mechanism.

Cold hitting warm and changing
to its upsweep, weeping

tree with its light tips
in the swamp.

(*Apeiron*
like the black-abyss/star-pocked screen-saver into which

all writing, all searched images
collapse) (You won't have—mama—

nowhere to stand)
(When the ether breaks)

Around the city lay a line of mold.

Of mildew, caked
filth, dried detritus, gas and shit, a paste of leaves
ground up and blackened. Of air-directed

waters—
Around the city was a line, a level
fluctuating mark.

                    (But there were no people)
                    (or Pampers or tampons) (or buses or cars)
                    (or electricity) (or vegetables) but there was

a boat, a floating
refrigerator turned on its back, with
two toddlers in it—

                    (I searched this image and could not
                    find it)
                    But there were people living everywhere.

All the people theorizing
from within their definite
substance in real time.

Under a livid
dome or trick
sky, under which

"the void
becomes a vortex"
once again—

[*Anarch.*]

Anarch., though, still.
Apeiron.

As she reminded us: going
to the underworld interminably on the subway.

Shades flit
through the broken station.

Their bodies rarefied
from white poison dust.

(The child insisted
he could not shit until his father's

disappearance was explained.
He drew a line

across the line that was carved into the bright
softness of his life.)

The intraquarky space, whose quality allegedly
is bliss.

(Not the veil, but the
lining of the veil.

The shimmering part the child swallows
as hardness in his gut, nervous tendrils

tying gut to brain, case
of the brain, its pulsing dark.

No government.
No buildings.
Anarch.

A simple knife in the hand, or a box of Pampers.)

"This article is about a cosmological theory. For the video game, see *Apeiron*. For the scientific journal, see *Apeiron*."

"For Pythagoras, the universe began as an apeiron, but at some point it inhaled the void from outside, filling the cosmos with bubbles that split the world. For Anaxagoras, apeiron rotated rapidly under control of a godlike *Nous*

(Mind), and the great speed of the rotation caused the universe to break—"

[*Then I dreamed of flying very low*]

Then I dreamed of flying very low in the bodily speed envelope
above a vast Mordor landscape, pitted carbon
and roiling red lava in the porous black. Hot wind

in the gesture of my face. In another chamber, tumid flowered paper
ribboning from sweating walls, and piles of brocade, rusted wrought-iron
chairs and bedsteads, muslin tissues, a veranda, something

tiered, extensive, ruined, and akin. The monster body
whose split apertures give onto a nauseous
vibrant ocean. Not the veil

but the lining of the veil.

Two (fathers/uncles) (brothers/strangers) wade in the
overflow. Hands steer the floating edges
of a doorless refrigerator.

"Cause you know—"

Deep soup of eddying
putrefaction. As bubbles spin and puncture
each diagram/the mind, their muscles

eat it. Glide through—as sky
rushes to touch structure, and water simultaneously
enters it. Density

of the real all fringed
with falsity. What kind
of shoes do they have on? To what high place

are they piloting their coffin-heavy doorless appliance
with children in it?
(A line drawn across

a softness made of water. Depthless

sunset, darkening
hot peach/robin's egg to ochre/gray-green.
Old used light in the room, a flaring

queasiness of light)—

Yes, of course
it is too double.

"Cause you know it's so hard
to love someone
when they do not love you."

[*Then falling upward*]

Then falling upward. Somersaulting azimuth

in the pupil. Hot wind

off the landslide, and I wrote in it, moved
its whorls around to inscribe a phrase
that started out polluted but got cleaner as it turned

into the fairy ship

(a chrysalid, a spirit-case)—

"No, that is a different
impossibility."

But persevering—

with painted prow and silken sails, expensive, delicate, a vehicle
more fluttering than an airplane
though likewise made of smoke, and how it came to be

cutting paths into the foam. Pearl
spume, horizon-eating
cloud, screen of the breast brought close

to be projected on, cream

slapping into/frothing from
the cave-mouth. Opal spill
of flame-retardant, spermicide, brain-matter.

The spirit-prow cuts zigzag paths that softly
part and fill, and undulating
zero flourishes. "Most thoughts

are unnecessary—"

[But there is more to constant transmission]

But there is more to constant transmission
than glass and wavelengths. First:

a distant heat
disturbing air. The noise heat

generates. And third:
bombardment

of swerving hitting
skin & bouncing

off, & simultaneously
infiltrating. Dazzled objects

seem to be slipping
slightly off

the convex, and children
would not like this landscape—

Thus I experienced

a headache day of light, a distant
point of sun rushing
close to fray the optic nerve, & a black spot

floating. Bone-rattling road
between long acreage
of yellow desert flower, hard-pan tesselated

with deep cracks, & a pilgrimage of minutes
sucking moisture from my tissues mixed
with gravity, laugh-tracks, incendiaries, altruism, energy-drink.

"World-mothering air—"

In the sewage/chocolate-milk flood
that is depth brought close & added to the street: unstrung
cable, car-parts, house-parts, tree-parts, obliterated

shapes, and bobbing empty plastic water bottles.
Two toddlers in their unplugged hard
appliance. Food and thought in their own

bodies bobbing is the body of the void/below
and on the surface guides
the streaming image. Droplets scatter

across their faces the surprisingly

large tonnage of a storm

With thanks to: W.H. Auden, Matthew Buckingham, Francis Cape, Brian Conley, Hélène Cixous, CNN, Ralph Waldo Emerson, Liz Fink, Nancy Holt, Google, Gerard Manley Hopkins, Son House, John Keats, Stanley Kunitz, Jaques Lacan, Led Zeppelin, Gordon Matta-Clark, Chazen Mellis, Ken Millet, Alice Notley, NPR, people in Afghanistan, people in airplanes, people in Iraq, people in Israel, people in meetings, people in New Orleans, people in Palestine, people in subway cars, people in the World Trade Center, Ezra Pound, Pete Seeger, Mary Shelley, Katrín Sigurdardóttir, Robert Smithson, J.R.R. Tolkien, Anne Waldman, Mark Wigley, Wikipedia.

This first edition, first printing, includes 26 limited edition copies signed by the author and lettered A-Z.

This book was set in Caslon, a typeface named after its designer, William Caslon, a British gunsmith and popular type designer of the mid-18th century. It is the first typeface of English origin and bears the distinction of being the typeface used to set the Declaration of Independence.